# *Goldie and Nin Adventures.*

Copyright © 2022.
Written and illustrated by Kristy Winter.
Yellow blossoms blooming through generations.

# Table of Contents

# Goldie

# Nin

# The Goldie and Nin Stories.

Ok, first of all I must introduce to you the notorious Goldie and Nin. They are two special fish that enlightened our world and will soon enlighten yours if you have not observed fish and all that they are, personality wise, I mean. Alright, let's see how to begin. Oh, yes. Let's start with Goldie the leader of the fish tank. She is like the mother, we will say. She loves to teach the new fish who come into her domain how to be super spoiled.

If you were a fish she would say, "Ok, this is what we do if you want more food. Watch me and you will see how it is done."

This is what she showed Nin our next fish who took it to a whole nother level. Alright, now to our first story.

# Nin and The Morning Adventures.

Ok, before I begin I must tell you I was sleeping and woke up to you know, do my number one and two business and the adventure begins when I come out of the bathroom.

"Alright, here I go, let's see if I can sneak past Nin and get some water to drink before going back to bed?"

By the way it is about 5:30am in the morning and yes, Nin is wide awake and is swimming.

"Hmm. Where is that human? I know she shows up about now and I know she'll try to sneak in here. Ha! I see you! Alright, its time human here I come!"

Nin jumps into the air and makes a giant splash.

Hmm. Where is that Human? I am hungry.
Kristy Winter 2022

"Awe man, he saw me! Now I have to feed him!"

5:30am
I see you she human. Feed me.
Man! He saw me!
Kristy Winter 2022.

Nin is  always hungry early in the morning and is fed by another he human, but sometimes the she human comes first and Nin always catches her sneaking and gets her to feed him.

"Alright, you caught me. Here you go."

"Thank you human. I love playing sneak and feed me. You aren't very good at this game, but I will let you think you have a chance!"

Then the he human comes in and sees Nin eating.

"Oh, you caught her again trying to sneak past you again, didn't you?"

Nin nods and finishes eating.

The he human says, "Hey, maybe you should let her think you didn't see her one of these times. Naa, it's too funny. Keep it up!"

# Goldie and Nin.

Let us begin with the day Goldie came into our fish tank. First of all, she is a goldfish, but she had prior knowledge from the pet store on how she was to be fed. She was introduced to our normal fish, mostly other goldfish. We put her into our fish tank and watched her adjust like we normally did. Of course after a period of a week or two some of the new fish would die off. Goldie stayed on and was named Goldie by the two smaller humans who watched them daily.

As she adjusted, we started to notice a different behavior in her than the other fish. She would go to the top of the water and jump up a little bit. The he human sometimes fed her extra when she did this. So, as any smart fish would, she recognized this and did it more often.  She continued to get fed a little more often and became a little bigger than the others. Then she would also look at the he human with her googly eyes and the he human started to feed her a little more.

More food
please.
Kristy
Winter 2000

She grew pretty big and took care of the other fish. One day a new fish had been in the other tank and had made it through the quarantine period. The he human thought it would be good to move this fish into Goldie's tank. The small humans called this fish Nin. At the time they did not know he was a koi fish. The he human placed Nin into Goldie's tank and immediately, they became friends. He swam with her a lot, she taught him her tricks, and the he human also fed him a little more.

Nin was different though. He grew much faster than Goldie and he had things hanging off of his mouth. The humans asked the pet store what type of fish he was. They said he was a koi fish and he could get very big. One day Nin was extra hungry and the he human had fed Nin the normal amount of food and Nin wanted more.

"I'm going to get his attention. Watch this Goldie!" Nin said.

Goldie looked at him and shook her head. Nin jumped up out of the tank and onto the table where the fish tank was.

"Whoa! What was that?

The he human turned around and saw Nin on the table.

"What are you doing? You need to be in your tank with water."

The he human carefully placed Nin back in the tank.

"What were you thinking, Nin?" Goldie said.

"I'm gonna do it again. Watch you'll see he'll feed me more."

Nin jumped high in the air and splashed some water on the table and Nin landed back in the tank.

"Are you hungry, Nin? You must be. Here is a little more, but that is all you get."

"What, I can't believe that worked Nin!" Goldie said.

# The Light Switch.

Let us begin with a normal day of Nin and Goldie swimming in the tank. It's about 5am in the morning. Nin and Goldie are swimming together as usual, when Nin gets an idea.

Nin looks at Goldie and says, "Let's try something new today, Goldie."

"Ok, I'll play along. You lead and I'll follow."

The he human walks into the room and turns on the light switch, which is located near the fish tank. The he human feeds the fish and goes about doing his normal routine. Nin jumps up into the air and flips the light switch off with his tail, lands back into the tank, and proceeds to act normal by swimming back and forth. The he human turns around and sees the light is off.

Let's see if the he human figures out, that I turned it off.
Kristy Winter 2022.

"Hmm. Better check the light bulb, maybe it burned out. Nope!"

The he human goes over to the light switch and sees the wall is wet.

"How did that water get there? Hmm. The light switch is off. Weird, I thought I turned it on. I bet the little ones turned it off out of habit after going to the bathroom."

The he human dries the wall off and turns the light switch back on. He then returns to his routine. Goldie and Nin look at each other with the orneriest look.

"Oh, yeah it's on!"

Kristy Winter 2022.

Goldie says, "My turn!"

She jumped up into the air did a flip and then smacked the light switch off and landed gracefully and gently back into the water. The he human turned around again and saw the light was off. This time he went directly to the light switch to see if it was turned off. It was and it was even more wet than last time. He dried the wall and the light switch.

"This is very odd indeed. The little ones are both asleep. So, it can't be them."

He turned the light switch on and off and back on again.

"Hmm. I wonder if the fish splashed water on the wall. I still don't know how the light switch went off. The fish didn't turn it off did they. Naa! So, weird."

He went back to doing his routine, but this time he would pay closer attention to the noises he heard. Goldie and Nin were laughing so hard that the water started sloshing back and forth.

Ha! Ha!
Ha! Ha!

The he human heard the water splashing and turned around. The light was on, but there was water on the floor.

"Hmm. That's weird. Nin is in the tank. So, I don't know."

The he human dried up the water and went back to his routine. Nin and Goldie continued to look at each other and laugh.

"Wow, we sure did confuse him," said Goldie.

"That was a lot of fun," said Nin.

"Do you want to try it one last time, Goldie?"

"I don't know he might catch us this time."

"I don't care if he catches me. I'd like to see his face," said Nin.

"Ok! Said Goldie.

Nin jumps up into the air and lightly flips the light switch off and lands back into the tank with a loud splash. The he human spins around and sees the water splash, but did not see Nin out of the tank.

"Oh, they must have jumped up and landed back in the water. That explains the water mess, but I still don't think they can turn the light switch off."

"Well, you'll never know he human will you. Ha, ha!" Said Goldie and Nin.

# The Little Humans.

"Hey, Nin. Do you want to mess with the little humans?"

"Ok, what do you want to do?"

"Ok, here's my thinking. The best time to mess with them is when they first wake up. Follow my lead."

"Ok! Nin said.

The she human woke the little ones and they rubbed their eyes and slowly crawled out of bed and proceeded to go do their bathroom number one or two business. As they came out of the bathroom one of the little humans felt a wet splash on their face. The little human looked up and around to see where the wetness might have came from.

"Huh, don't see anything and my sister is still in the bathroom. Oh, well."

Where's the water coming from?
Time to wake up!
Kristy Winter 2022.

Nin and Goldie began to giggle. The second little human came out of the bathroom and also felt a wetness on her face. Her sister had already gone to make her bed so it wasn't her.

"Hmm. That's weird. Oh, well."

By this time Goldie and Nin were laughing so hard that the water started to slosh out of the fish tank. The little ones heard the splashing water and ran out of their room.

"The water came from the fish tank. I never would have guessed," said the two little humans.

"Oh, it's Nin and Goldie! We caught you!"

Nin and Goldie stopped laughing and looked at the little humans. They both gave them the googly eyes, saying not us.

The little humans said, "Nice try, but we know you did it!"

Then Goldie swam to the top of the tank and said, "Of course we did. You looked so sleepy we just had to wake you up."

The two little humans looked at each other and said, "Did Goldie just talk?"

"That's right!" Goldie said.

The little humans got quiet and walked over to the tank.

"Wow, that's amazing! Please don't splash us anymore." Said the little humans.

"Ok, as long as you get us some extra food every now and then when we ask." said Nin.

"Ok, but promise to keep talking to us."

"Alright!" Nin and Goldie said.

# *The Surprise at Night.*

This story begins when all the lights went out and the humans went to sleep. Meanwhile, in the fish tank, Nin and Goldie are swimming together.

A new fish called Fishybusiness said, "Alright, the humans are asleep it's time! Turn on the spinning colorful lights and set that bass music! Party is my name, let's go!"

The lights turn on, twist and flash, and the bass music is bumpin'. Nin and Goldie are swaying and twisting. Fishybusiness jumps up out of the tank and flips and lands back into the tank. Nin spins in circles around and around and Goldie shakes her tail as though she has on a fancy dress on. Fishybusiness shakes his head and bounces to the beat.

"Work it! Yeah! Go Nin and Goldie!" Said Fishybusiness.

Shake it Goldie!
It's time to party!
Kristy Winter 2022.

Nin and Goldie jump out of the tank and over each other and land back in the tank.

All are having fun when all of a sudden a sleepy little one walks to the bathroom and sees flashing lights and the fish swaying and twisting.

"Whoa, am I seeing this?" Said the little one.

She goes to the bathroom and comes back out. She still sees the fish moving the same way and walks closer to the tank. She starts to hear music and starts to dance with the fish.

Meanwhile, her sister wakes up and peeks around the corner and sees her sister and the fish dancing.

"Dance party! Yeah!"

She begins to dance as well. All are having so much fun they don't hear the she human walking over to them.

"Alright, girls you've had your fun. You have to go to school in the morning. Turn the lights and music off it's time for bed."

The girls tell the fish to turn the music and lights off and say goodnight. The little humans go to bed.

"Wow, I wonder if they do that every night?"

"I don't know, but it sure was fun."

The she human looks at the tank and says, "I wonder if the girls started that dance party or if it was the fish. Hmm. I guess I'll never know. Goodnight fish. If I was you, I'd try to keep it down. We don't want to wake the he human."

"Alright, she human. Don't forget to come feed us at 5:30am."

# How to Be a Ninja 101.

"Ok, fish. You are here because you are ready to become ninjas. Alright, the first test is to see if you can flip and land on top of the side of the tank. Ok, let me demonstrate."

The other fish watch and then try to do the same.

"Ok, don't forget to make sure you are not seen by the humans, unless you are trying to freak them out."

All nod and continue to watch and listen.

"For our next test you must jump up in the air, land on the table, and then flop yourself back into the tank."

Flipping out and back into the tank technique.
Kristy Winter 2022.

Goldie continues to demonstrate and test the fish to see if they are ready to become ninja fish.

"Ok, for the last test you have to do three flips up in the air and then touch the ceiling. Then come back down into the water gracefully with a small splash."

Touch the Ceiling technique.
Kristy Winter 2022.

Most of the fish passed and some didn't. The ones who didn't pass were taught how to turn light switches off with their tails.

"Alright, good job everyone. Now let's see if you can pass the human test? I will ask one of you each week to do something when the human walks past our tank. The trick is not to get caught. If you pass this test you are officially a ninja. If not we will continue until you pass or decide you are done."

The first week, Goldie had a fish do a back flip and land gracefully back into the water after the human walked by the tank. The fish passed with flying colors. The second week, Goldie had a fish jump up and touch the ceiling and then land back into the tank without being heard. This fish passed of course. The third week, she had a fish jump into the air and land on the side of the tank, but this fish wanted to freak out the human. So, it stayed in its stance until the human turned around and then jumped into the tank.

The human wiped their eyes and said, "That didn't just happen. I think I'm seeing things."

The he human walked away and shook his head.

"That was close! Good job for freaking out the human." Said Goldie.

Hello human!
That didn't just happen, did it?
You did a great job!
Yeah! I totally freaked him out!
My fish do the strangest things.
Kristy Winter 2022

# The Ninja Transition.

"Alright, you have obviously passed your ninja training, so we will now begin the real training. Please grab a water suit and put it on. We will now proceed to the basement for your official training."

Everyone who passed put their water suits on, jumped out of the tank, and walked to the wall.

"Alright, follow me and be as quiet as you can." Said Goldie.

They slithered down the hallway and flipped down the steps to the basement. When they got to the basement, they saw other fish in water suits kicking, punching, and flipping. There were even fish throwing shurikens and lifting weights.

Ninja Watersuit
Training
Kristy Winter
2022.

"Wow! Now this is training."

Goldie continued to train each of them and showed them how to breathe without the water suits.

"Now only do this in emergencies in case you get stuck on the floor and only for ten minutes. You must get back into the water before ten minutes or you may dehydrate and die."

All practiced and listened closely. Then a door creaking sound was heard. A little human went into the basement.

"Hide everyone quick over here!"

"I thought I heard something. Oh, well, back upstairs."

"That was close. Everyone back to the tank. Tomorrow will be a vigorous training day." Said Goldie.

I hope you enjoyed the Goldie, Nin, and Fishybusiness stories. You just never know what they will do next. Take care and continue to see the world in different ways.